FIFE

Edited by Allison Dowse

First published in Great Britain in 1999 by
YOUNG WRITERS
Remus House,
Coltsfoot Drive,
Woodston,
Peterborough, PE2 9JX
Telephone (01733) 890066

HB ISBN 0 75431 520 7
SB ISBN 0 75431 521 5

FOREWORD

Poetry Now Young Writers have produced poetry books in conjunction with schools for over eight years; providing a platform for talented young people to shine. This year, the Celebration 2000 collection of regional anthologies were developed with the millennium in mind.

With the nation taking stock of how far we have come, and reflecting on what we want to achieve in the future, our anthologies give a vivid insight into the thoughts and experiences of the younger generation.

We were once again impressed with the quality and attention to detail of every entry received and hope you will enjoy the poems we have decided to feature in *Celebration 2000 Fife* for many years to come.

CONTENTS

Inverkeithing Primary School

Stacey Brierley	30
Liam Burnett	31
Darren Coutts	32
Ryan Cunningham	33
Andrew Jude	34
Danielle Lumsden	35
Brian Reid	36
Scott MacDonald	37
Aisling Adamson	38
Claire McIntosh	39
Samantha Rennie	40
Debbie Wright	41
Scott Crichton	42
Eric Dey	43
Dahl Palfrey	44
Daryl Leonard	45

Kinghorn Primary School

Fiona Speed	46
Heather Stewart	47
Rebecca Molden	48
Scott Shepherd	49
David McGuire	50
Ross Stewart	51
Claire Dalzell	52
Kylie Hourston	53
Martyn Rollo	54

Newburgh Primary School

Laurie Burnett	55
Andrew Lennie	56
Stephanie Lawrence	57
Yvette Udall	58
Toni Allan	59
Kirsty Eadie	60
Shona McGregor	61
Danielle Trainer	62

Cheryl Robertson	63
Laura K McNae	64
Stacie Mackenzie	65
Kevin Sargent	66
Andrew Macdonald	67
Kyle Noble	68
Jade Wells	69

St Brides RC Primary School

Christopher Black	70
Kurtis Wood	71
Jenny Knox	72
Rachael Spowart	73
Natalie Adamson	74

St Joseph's Primary School, Kelty

Laura Almond	75
Danielle Somerville	76
Yvonne McCaskill	77
Katy-Louise West	78
Ashleigh McDougall	79
Claire Ednie	80
Samantha McCulloch	81
Jason Moffatt	82
James Gill	83
Claire Donaldson	84
Megan Webb	85

St Katharine's School, St Andrews

Virginia Cayzer	86
Emily Ventress	87
Hilary Myles	88
Katrina Nancy Larson	89
Rachael Drummond	90
Lynnette Nicholson	91
Emma Barclay	92
Merle Henderson	93
Poppy Open	94

The Poems

A DAY IN THE HEDGEROW

Hedgerows, a blaze of colour,
A breeze is stirring the leaves,
A light green briar all bathed in gold,
When the sun comes up.

Speedy beetles busy looking for food,
Butterflies like darts of colour,
Among the flowering plants,
All beautiful in the midday light.

Hawthorn so spiky and fierce,
Blackberries juicy and tasty,
Especially in a jam,
All shadowy at dusk.

Peter Nurick (9)
Cleish Primary School

THE BUSHY HEDGEROW

The bushy hedgerow in the countryside,
The beech with its royal and shiny leaves,
The bumble-bee going to the thistle with his purple crown,
His neighbour the dandelion with his big yellow head,
Down below, the rabbits run in and out of the hedgerow.

Dale Carver (10)
Cleish Primary School

MR UNFIT AND MR FIT

Mr Unfit

I eat lots of chocolate while watching TV,
I go to bed late, at half past three,
I have a smoke until eight at night,
And I think I'm really fit.

Mr Fit

I run half a marathon every day,
I eat four bananas while reading a book,
I go to bed early every night,
I know I'm really fit.

I skip and jump every day,
I go swimming three times a week,
I love to play basketball,
And now I'm really fit.

David Fairbairn *(8)*
Cleish Primary School

HEDGE

The autumn hedge has a golden yellow jacket,
In the bushy dense core climbers are twisting,
The ivy is curling around the undergrowth,
Where a mouse enjoys the juicy taste of the brambles,
Rose bay-willow herb with the elephant hawk moth,
Caterpillar eating freely,
A small vole is foraging for food under the fallen brown leaves.

Calum Hill (12)
Cleish Primary School

THE HAIRY CAR

I heard a tale
Of a hairy car.
The cliff road was slippery.
Darkness.
Nothing in sight.
On a rock,
Beside the road,
Lay a gun.
Headlights shone on metal,
A lethal weapon.
The driver felt fear,
Braked too fast,
Skidded off the cliff road,
The cliff road.

Stuart Wallace (8)
Commercial Primary School

TREES

There are beech trees,
Oak trees,
Elm trees too.
Climbing trees is fun,
If you don't know what to do.

Maples come from Canada,
You won't find one here,
But if you look very closely
One might appear.

Holly trees have spiky leaves,
They have red berries too,
Trees make beds for animals,
And my bedhead too.

Sarah Alexander (8)
Commercial Primary School

THE DANCING TREE

Green tree
Dancing neatly
Turning round like a ballerina
Pointing neatly
As sweetly as can be
Little lambs jumping
The tree dancing neatly
Neatly as can be.

Joanna Coull (8)
Commercial Primary School

THE SECRET

A secret is hard to keep,
You can't even let out a peep,
And if you decide to let it out,
Do it in a whisper,
Not a shout.
If someone tells you one,
Keep it a secret,
Or your friendship will be gone,
I'll tell you a secret that beats the rest,
I think secrets are the best! Shhh . . .

Laura Davidson (9)
Commercial Primary School

CAN YOU KEEP A SECRET?

Can you keep a secret, if I tell you one?
Can you keep a secret if I tell you right now?
Can you keep a secret if I tell you later?
Sorry, you can't have my secret, it's mine!

Katie Sneddon (8)
Commercial Primary School

TREES

I went to the woods and there I saw squirrels, climbing the trees.
I saw butterflies resting on leaves.
I saw all the adult squirrels getting some berries for their kids.
When I went to the woods I saw a bird's nest on the twigs.

Gillian Buchanan (8)
Commercial Primary School

TREES

T rees, waving about in the breeze.
R ough bark all the way up.
E very leaf papery and crunchy.
E very tree blessed with beauty.
S un helps it grow to touch the sky.

Hannah-Rose Livingstone (8)
Commercial Primary School

TREES

Some trees are tall and some are small.
Some are fat and some are thin.
Some are pretty but some are dull.
But I don't care, for I love them all.

Lorraine Livingstone (8)
Commercial Primary School

TREES

Trees sing in the spring,
Trees dance in the summer,
Trees wriggle in the autumn,
Trees celebrate in the winter,
Trees easily fall asleep in the cold winter breezes.

Claire Simpson (8)
Commercial Primary School

THE APPLE TREE

I walked into the orchard and I saw the branches twist.
The twigs were lumpy with buds.
The blossom started to drop pink petals.
The petals looked like snow.
The apples were so juicy
And then I went home.

Laura Seymour (8)
Commercial Primary School

SUMMER'S BREEZE

Summer's breeze is as cool as ice,
is very nice,
can beat the rain,
can make you feel the pain,
can blow you away,
when it is May.

Natalie Howie (8)
Commercial Primary School

HALLOWE'EN

On Hallowe'en
the spooks come out to
jump about
the street.
They roar all night
And creak and bite
and even trick
or
treat.

Paul Haddow (8)
Commercial Primary School

SECRET

I have a secret
that's close to my heart.
I have a secret
from which I'll never part.
I have a secret
that's special to me.
I hid my secret in the Secrets Tree.

Lynsey Mackay (8)
Commercial Primary School

THE PARK

There once was a man called John
Who had a son called Shaun.
They went to the park,
and heard a dog bark.
They went on a swing,
and heard someone sing.
They went on the slide,
and saw someone hide.
And then they went home.

Lorna Douglas (8)
Commercial Primary School

A SECRET

I like secrets,
They are really good,
Because they always put me
In a good mood.

I like secrets,
Because they let you know,
What you don't already know!

Samantha Callan (8)
Commercial Primary School

THE HUNTED HUNTER

He crept through the jungle, alone with his gun
Looking for some animals, hoping for some fun
That's when he heard it, the deafening sound
The sound of lions ready to pounce.

Upon him they jumped
It must have been sore
The hunter, he died
I will say no more.

Alisdair Campbell (9)
Commercial Primary School

MONSTER TRUCK

A monster truck
racing through the forest.
It was going fast.
Its engine was roaring,
It was going over the bumps easily and smoothly.
Some day I wish I could ride the mechanical monster
And feel as if,
I'm controlling . . .
The whole . . .
World!

Duncan Tweedie (8)
Commercial Primary School

THE MIND OF SECRETS

I hate secrets, I hate secrets.
Trees' secrets,
Computer secrets,
Family secrets,
I *hate* secrets.

Clare Gavine (8)
Commercial Primary School

SECRETS

Secrets aren't very nice
They are horrible,
They are rude,
They are nasty,
They hurt people's feelings
They can be threats,
They are frightening.

Callum McNeill (8)
Commercial Primary School

THE CHRISTMAS TREE

When
it's   time
to   decorate
the   Christmas
tree   my   mum
calls us to decorate
it with the crackers
and all the other things.
When   it's
done we switch
on the lights and we switch
it off and go to our rooms
to wait for Father Christmas.

Scott Johnston (8)
Commercial Primary School

TARTAN

Tartan is the kilt my dad
wore on his wedding day.

Tartan is the colour of
the pencil you use.

Tartan is the colour of
the T-shirt you wear.

Tartan is the colour you
paper your room with.

Tartan is the colour of
the pencil case you use.

Tartan is the colour of the
tie you wear.

Tartan is the colour of your
hair when you dye it.

Tartan is the colour
of your hat.

Michael Hastie (11)
Dunino Primary School

ALISON'S POEM

As cold as iced water
as hard as a brick wall.

As white as a scary ghost
as sharp as a razor.

As bright as the sun
as old as my great grandparents.

As keen as my brother
as black as a witch.

As smooth as my dog's fur
as cool as an iced drink.

As good as my puppy.

As weird as water, brick, razor, ghost, sun,
parents, brother, witch, fur, drink, puppy.

Alison Laird (11)
Dunino Primary School

STREAM

The water flows down the stream
Makes a lovely noise
When it flows down the stream
      It's cold
      It's nice
      It's a stream.

Malcolm Mitchell (10)
Dunino Primary School

SPRING

S pring comes with daffodils growing
P eople come who are lawn mowing
R abbits come out to play
I t is spring, it's spring today
N owhere is a sign of snow
G ood people become friend not foe.

Marissa Wilson (8)
Dunino Primary School

MY MUM

My mum is the kind of mum whom I love very much,
because she's the kind of mum who:
Cooks my dinner,
Buys me cool clothes,
Gives me lots of pocket money,
Helps me paint my nails,
Gives me a hand with homework,
Lets me have sleepovers,
Talks to me when she is upset,
Stands up for me when I'm in trouble,
Lets me wear make-up
And will love me for ever!

Lisa Houston (11)
Dunino Primary School

IN THE PIT

Black faces, sore hands,
Crooked back! No!
Rich people watch us suffer,
They don't care, they only want the money,
We get paid two shillings,
Last week a girl died down here,
She was only 10 years old,
When she died, the manager said
'More money for me!'
I work in the pit.

Stacey Brierley (10)
Inverkeithing Primary School

POOR LITTLE CREATURE

Lonely,
Starving,
Needs some help,
Has no parents,
No one to help him,
No one,
At all.

Liam Burnett (11)
Inverkeithing Primary School

THE POOR

Poor,
Not rich,
On the streets,
No one to love,
No one to love,
No one to care for,
Fighting for life,
Just won't starve,
Very poor,
Life.

Darren Coutts (10)
Inverkeithing Primary School

POOR

O ne day I was selling matches,
R ight then I got my shirt caught on a nail,
P oor people have ripped clothes,
H ave never seen the world,
A ll they time they have to work,
N ever have time.

Ryan Cunningham (10)
Inverkeithing Primary School

MATCHSTICK BOY

Lonely
Freezing feet
Screaming for money
Sleeping on the streets
Get your matchsticks here!
No home for me
Desperate
Starving
Young.

Andrew Jude (10)
Inverkeithing Primary School

A POOR LITTLE BEGGAR

Cold little beggar in the street,
Looking for something good to eat,
Sore little toes, sore little feet,
Crunching around in the freezing cold sleet.
Don't want to go to the workhouse,
Don't want to climb any chimneys,
I hate living in the street.

Danielle Lumsden (10)
Inverkeithing Primary School

THE BULLY AND ME

Me

A big bully hurting my friends,
Bullies calling me names,
That bully is after me,
Fear on my tongue,
I hit the bully, he hit me back!

The Bully

People running away from me,
People saying 'Please don't hurt me,'
People's blood running cold,
Fresh air and sweat on my tongue,
I see that person, he will say,
'Now I'm getting my own back!'

Brian Reid (10)
Inverkeithing Primary School

MINE

Pushing and pulling,
The big carts of coal,
The men of the mine,
Work very, very hard,
As trappers
And cart-pushers,
They work very hard.
Because it's early to bed,
And early to rise,
It makes them work hard,
And be 'Worldly Wise'.

Scott MacDonald (10)
Inverkeithing Primary School

THE BEGGAR

Begging in the streets,
Nothing good for them to eat!
They always have bare feet,
Shivering in their rags!
Saying 'Flowers for sale
Children in need.'

Aisling Adamson (10)
Inverkeithing Primary School

I'M AN ORPHAN

I'm an orphan,
Cold and bare,
I stand in the streets,
While the rich people stare,
I feel sad for I have no home,
So in the streets
I have to roam.

In the streets I have to sell,
Beautiful posies,
And bright red roses.

I'm an orphan,
Cold and bare,
I stand in the streets
While the rich people stare.

Claire McIntosh (10)
Inverkeithing Primary School

A COMPUTER RAP

Plug me in
Switch me on
Press the button
I'll sing a song
Come into Computer Land
I'm begging you, I demand
Take me into your mind
Forge ahead, don't stay behind.

Samantha Rennie (11)
Inverkeithing Primary School

NO ONE TO CARE

All frail and weak, standing on the street,
Rough leathery skin and sore bare feet,
A tear-stained face,
So desperate for money,
Wishing just for once she could be rich.

Shuffling along the pavement, lonely and sad,
Feeling envious of those who have love and a caring family,
At the end of the day, this starving, unwanted flower seller goes away.
Feeling that life has somehow cheated on her . . .

Debbie Wright (10)
Inverkeithing Primary School

TOUGH LUCK

Skin and bones, no sleep at all,
For his starving little body,
He coughs and splutters all day long,
He looks so sad with his desperate eyes,
His clothes are sooty and darkened,
He looks out of a window with envy,
And imagines a better world,
Of course, he's a chimney sweep, sad and lonely.

Scott Crichton (11)
Inverkeithing Primary School

THE BEGGAR

Deafened by the noise,
Choked by the steam,
Filthy and ragged,
Moneyless and starving,
Skin and bone, no food to eat,
Orphaned at an early age,
No home for him in no-man's land,
A poor beggar living on the street,
No shoes to cover his frozen feet,
Soon even his shadow will disappear.

Eric Dey (10)
Inverkeithing Primary School

COMPUTERS/HUMANS

What would we do without them?
They back up our files.
Some come with CD drives
What would we do without them?
They give us good care
They teach us things
I'm glad I have one
We need each other.

Dahl Palfrey (10)
Inverkeithing Primary School

SUPER SYSTEM

I am a mastermind,
I am a super system,
I am virtual reality,
I am nothing without man.
I am a whizz wonder,
I am a homework helper,
I am an electronic city,
I am a zapping inspiration,
I am your link to the Internet,
I am a powerful god,
I am a *computer!*

Daryl Leonard (10)
Inverkeithing Primary School

ROBIN

Getting ready for its flight
It's very high in height.
Spotting food
In the wood.
That sounds like my robin.

Beautiful wings
Beautiful feathers
Flying through the air.
Gliding, squawking and singing.
That sounds like my robin.

This bird does not dive
Of course it's a robin.
Zooming, whizzing
In the air
Flying, soaring
That sounds like my robin.

Fiona Speed (9)
Kinghorn Primary School

IN YOUR IMAGINATION

In your imagination you can walk on water,
You can swim in a chocolate sea.
You can land on the sun,
And you can turn into a bumble-bee.

Just imagine . . .

Heather Stewart (10)
Kinghorn Primary School

IMAGINARY THINGS

Come to a place of imaginary things
Fly over rooftops, soar over seas.
You can travel the world whilst lying in your bed.
Experience the past, present and future.
Zoom into fairy tales made years ago.

Turn into objects that are out of this world.
Fly to the moon and back.
Break your arm or leg but don't get hurt.
In this land of imagination.
Rule the world and the seas.

Rebecca Molden (10)
Kinghorn Primary School

CONFLICT

C is for the crying of the nations
O is for old war memories
N is for never again
F is for fighting enemy countries
L is for loss of life
I is for invincible, but the armies aren't,
C is for cruise missiles
T is for total devastation.

Scott Shepherd (12)
Kinghorn Primary School

CONFLICT

C is for conquering domination of the five continents.
O is for offence, breaking the rules.
N is for negligence of the innocent people who get killed.
F is for fighting, killing for the battle of power,
L is for lacking in the knowledge of peace and happiness.
I is for infantry, soldiers who risk their lives.
C is for coffins for the people who were killed at war,
T is for tanks driving through the battlefield.

David McGuire (11)
Kinghorn Primary School

CONFLICT

C ourageous soldiers going to war,
O ffering no mercy to enemy units,
N o opposition must survive,
F ill in the battlefield with no unity,
L ying in bed and thinking about,
I ll and dying soldiers being badly hurt,
C ruising bombers overhead ready,
T o kill more innocent men.

Ross Stewart (11)
Kinghorn Primary School

CONFLICT

C is for cover from the bombs
O is for our family who are threatened by war
N is for nations joining together
F is for flags waving in the wind
L is for losses equal on both sides
I is for an idea of where everything is
C is for countdown till wars die out
T is for time till we stop it.

Claire Dalzell (11)
Kinghorn Primary School

CONFLICT

C is for conquering courage.
O is for official aircraft.
N is for never-ending bombs.
F is for frightful enemies.
L is for lasting lives.
I is for the injured.
C is for captured people.
T is for terrified children.

Kylie Hourston (11)
Kinghorn Primary School

CONFLICT

C is for concerned relatives back at home
O ur family in amongst the victims
N o cease in the firing of bullets
F ire another cruise missile
L ike it's never going to end
'I hate this war'
C onflict like this should be stopped
T oday would be perfect.

Martyn Rollo (11)
Kinghorn Primary School

CELEBRATION 2000

Millennium is near
Parties are here
Food, games, presents and beer.
Celebration worldwide from Nigeria to the river Clyde
Millennium worries are also here like the bug
No not an insect, the computer bug.
When the clock strikes midnight we will all be hoping
For peace all around
More cars will be thought of and
More bought from the big manufacturers
More will be made
Better treatment will be of aid
In 2000.

Laurie Burnett (11)
Newburgh Primary School

MILLENNIUM 2000

M illennium comes every thousand years,
I   t could be full of memories,
L ots of people will be shedding tears,
L ots of people will be thinking of stories,
E vents in the past,
N ew babies will be born.
N ew ideas
I   n the millennium,
U FOs might appear,
M e, I don't know what to think.

S urprises happening, hopes for world peace,
U niting people, helping homeless,
R oad parties,
P arties in houses, music blaring out,
R ebirth of Kurt Cobain
I   mprovement in rock music,
S pirits visiting
E arth
S aving the rainforest, in the *millennium!*

Andrew Lennie (11)
Newburgh Primary School

CELEBRATION 2000

It's one minute to twelve,
The streets are quiet,
The pubs are quiet,
Everywhere's quiet.

People thinking what's going to happen
In one minutes time,
Is there going to be nobody on the streets?
In the houses partying, drinking beer,
Listening to pop music.

Is there going to be a Millennium Bug?
What's it going to destroy,
Our house or even the whole Earth?

Is there going to be an improvement
With our transport system?

Are there going to be aliens in our houses?

Is there going to be a planet invasion?

Is it going to be a better world?

Stephanie Lawrence (11)
Newburgh Primary School

MILLENNIUM 2000

In the year 2000 the millennium will come,
I thought by now we would be more civilised,
Of course we are, but what about the wars still being caused?
Innocent people dying just because they are
A different colour or believe in a different God.

On the other hand there will be parties all through the day
On New Year's Eve.
Some people will even be celebrating the rebirth of God,
Others think aliens will come.

Will animals be out of the danger of extinction?
What about all the beautiful creatures that will be lost?
Our expanding cities could mean that one day
Our children will only be able to look at pictures
Of extinct animals and the way things used to be.

Yvette Udall (11)
Newburgh Primary School

2000

The year 2000 will be a year of joy,
for every little girl and boy,
celebration, music, discos and food,
people will be having fun,
but what about the Millennium Bug?
Will we be invaded by aliens?
World tragedy, death,
will the planet blow up or will we be crushed?
Will the world come to an end,
will there be better homes?
World peace would make for better lives,
which in turn would make a better world.
Or will our countries continue
to go to war?

Toni Allan (11)
Newburgh Primary School

CELEBRATION 2000

In the year 2000 there's more to come,
You never know you might have fun.
People having parties all night long,
You'll never get to sleep with all the songs.
Nobody should really be in their bed,
They should be out partying instead.
People drinking having fun,
There's lots of food to fill your tum,
All the hopes for the millennium.

Kirsty Eadie (11)
Newburgh Primary School

2000

Year 2000 what does it mean,
Aliens, pollution, World War III.
Another thousand years waved goodbye,
Another thousand years come in sight,
Planet invasion help me please!

Year 2000 what does it mean?
Millennium home, Millennium Dome,
Capital city, streets of gold,
A thousand stories have been told,
Space travel may be fun,
But saving animals is more crucial!

Year 2000 parties galore,
Celebrations,
Food for all.

Shona McGregor (11)
Newburgh Primary School

PLANET 2000

What does it mean,
What does it mean,
To let the planet lose its green?
What does it do,
What does it do,
To put animals in the zoo?

Who really cares,
Who really cares,
About the bees, the birds and the bears?
Who really knows,
Who really knows,
About the care for nature we should show?

Are we mad,
Are we mad,
To let the Earth get so bad?

No one knows what millennium will bring,
Worries hopes and lots of strange things.
Will the panda become extinct?
Will dolphins be on the brink?
Nature is wonderful, nature is good,
So let nature be how it should.

Danielle Trainer (11)
Newburgh Primary School

CELEBRATION 2000

Is the millennium really worth it
Millions of pounds have been spent
In the end where's it all gone?
The Millennium Bug is here
Are the aliens really near?

At the end of '99
It's going to be a special time
As next year is the millennium
Time for celebration and fun,
Whether you're at the Millennium Dome
Or being with friends at your home.

Cheryl Robertson (12)
Newburgh Primary School

CELEBRATION 2000

M illennium comes every thousand years,
I t could be full of surprises,
L ots of people will be having fun,
L onging for world peace and better homes,
E xploring new things,
N o more work at school,
N o more cruelty to animals,
I llness will cause death,
U p up and away to space,
M illennium Bug will come.

Laura K McNae (11)
Newburgh Primary School

CELEBRATION 2000

M ost people will be celebrating
I   llnesses will be cured
L ots of people will be partying
L ots of places will be lit up
E vents in the future
N o more suffering
N o more cruelty to animals
I   nvitations handed out for space travel
U FOs land on Earth
M illennium is coming soon.

C ome and join the fun
E njoying new things
L ying in bed with a hangover
E xciting events
B eer, lager, vodka and don't forget the brandy
R ushed off your feet making everything special
A fter 12 strike 2000
T en, nine, eight, seven, six, five, four, three, two, one, 2000
I   n the future not in the past
O nwards to see what it holds
N ew beginnings, new people, new friends!

Stacie Mackenzie (12)
Newburgh Primary School

THE MILLENNIUM

The millennium is nearly here,
So let's make the best of this year,
As in the year 2000,
Not everything will be sound,
Global warming and the Millennium Bug,
Are just a couple of problems,
Computers may crash, electronics may smash,
And we may have to start from scratch,
But not everything will be doom and gloom,
As into the year 2000 we zoom.
Parties, discos all day long,
From midnight when we hear *ding dong!*
From firework displays to celebrations,
It might bring together all the nations!
At last we might have peace on Earth
Until the next millennium.

Kevin Sargent (11)
Newburgh Primary School

CELEBRATION 2000

The millennium is near,
Some things are to fear,
The Millennium Bug is one,
Aliens and UFOs are another,
There's a good side as well,
It could be full of celebration,
People drinking and partying all night,
But people have hopes,
World peace is what most people want,
But it's all about another 1000 years in the past,
So it's all down to the bells to ring for '99
To be in the past.

Andrew Macdonald (12)
Newburgh Primary School

2000

Millennium Dome
Me at home
Space travel
Mysteries unravel
Maybe we'll be glad
Maybe we'll be sad
Who knows,
Who knows?

Think of the happiness
Think of the sadness
Who knows,
Who knows?

Millennium Bug
Computer viruses
All the troubles we have
What will happen?

Faster technology
Than ever before
Will we have to start again?

Kyle Noble (11)
Newburgh Primary School

CELEBRATION 2000

The millennium is coming closer,
I hear clocks and music going round in my head,
People drinking and having fun, time just flies by.
I hope that we will get world peace and not war!
Maybe we could have a better world
We could have a world tragedy,
Or will there be a sudden death, I don't know.
Warning, warning it's the Millennium Bug
Try to move away quickly!
There might even be an alien invasion
And they will take over the planet.
Some people would like a new kind of transport
Like solar powered cars
Or maybe even a new type of housing.
Whatever it is, people flying about in solar powered cars,
To a nice peaceful world.
I just want to say have a great millennium

And like Robbie Williams says,
'We've got stars directing our fate
And we're praying it's not too late,
Cos we're falling from grace
Millennium'.

Jade Wells (11)
Newburgh Primary School

CELEBRATION 2000

All the people rushing home
for the millennium.
Coming home for the
Edinburgh street party two thousand.
Fireworks light up the sky
the clock on the castle walls
fills the people's hearts
because when it comes to zero
everyone gives a big cheer
because the millennium is here.
All the people shout with joy
they throw themselves about like a rubber toy.
If all the people drink too much
they'll throw up all over their bus.
2000 is going to be a great year
when all the people shout and cheer.
So when the clock strikes twelve
all the people shout and yell
'Hip hip hurrah!
Hip hip hurrah!'

Christopher Black (9)
St Brides RC Primary School

CELEBRATION 2000

Here we go into a new 100 years
With people having parties now and every day
Computers near and far crashing now and then
The lights are going out
So we can't move about
Watch all that happens inside and out
And watch all the computers
You might be in for a *surprise*
Get out the streamers and poppers
And party quick, quick, quick.

All prepare for a *celebration* not to be forgotten
With young or old, a party for everyone
People cry with laughter, with joy or with sadness
So let's begin a new century and life
We'll have to light some candles
Maybe six or seven
Soon we'll begin to think
About the Millennium Dome
People just can't wait
Until the clocks strike twelve.

Fireworks shoot up in colourful sparks
Lighting the dull Millennium Dome
Let's begin our decorations
And all the things that make it happy
Watch near and far
At all the people with fireworks
But most of all enjoy your millennium celebration.

Kurtis Wood (9)
St Brides RC Primary School

CELEBRATION 2000?

Is my world going to end
Or is it just the beginning,
Who knows?
Is my world going to improve
Or is it going to get worse
Who knows?
The thing I would hope for
In the year 2000
Is for the world to live in
Peace, love
And harmony.

Jenny Knox (9)
St Brides RC Primary School

CELEBRATION 2000

The year 2000 is coming hip hip hooray
With all the adults laughing and shouting
And the old people talking away.

The year 2000 is coming hip hip hooray
The children will be glad
The adults happy and gay.

The year 2000 is coming hip hip hooray
Time to say goodbye
But that's all I can say!
Happy New Year!

Rachael Spowart (9)
St Brides RC Primary School

CELEBRATION 2000

100 years ago, right now today,
I was another century away.
I couldn't sing, I couldn't walk,
I couldn't run, I couldn't talk.
Now I'm older and I understand,
That life is sometimes good or bad.

100 years ago, right now today,
I didn't know if my world was to stay.
I wasn't here, but now I am,
So let's celebrate now the best that we can
In 1999 it was OK
But year 2000 is one day away.

100 years ago, right now today
My life was not very gay
But the year 2000 goes bang in your face
I marvel at its amazing grace
That God took the time,
To make our wonderful world.

100 years ago, right now today
I thought of an amazing way
To look forward,
And also see,
Our year 2000.

Natalie Adamson (10)
St Brides RC Primary School

MY TEDS ON MY BED

I have a teddy called Ted
He's small and cuddly
And sleeps on my bed.

His friend is Wee Ted
Who is smaller than Ted
Wee Ted is white and red.

Wee Ted and Ted, every day are fed
They're hungry and thirsty
For honey and bread.

Laura Almond (10)
St Joseph's Primary School, Kelty

MILLENNIUM

The millennium is here
So let's give a cheer
And we're ringing the bells for the new year.

Some children drink cola
And the adults drink beer
Three cheers to the millennium and the new year.

Some bangers go pop
And the children all yell
We've made a new start for the millennium year.

Danielle Somerville (10)
St Joseph's Primary School, Kelty

MY CAT AND MY RAT

Bobby is my cat
Splinter is my rat
they fight all day
they never play
especially on Wednesday.
No matter what I do or say
they fight and fight every day
I don't care if they fight or play
I'll always love them for
eternity.

Yvonne McCaskill (10)
St Joseph's Primary School, Kelty

MY MUM

I go 'Mum'
and her recipes are yum
But I do love my mum.

My mum is my mum
because I will never leave her
And she will never leave me.

My mum is my mum
because she loves me and
I love her.

Katy-Louise West (9)
St Joseph's Primary School, Kelty

CLOSE FRIENDS

Everyone needs friends,
the reason never ends,
some people go away,
but good friends will always stay.

In your hour of need,
you need good friends indeed,
happiness is not far away,
when you see your friends every day.

Ashleigh McDougall (9)
St Joseph's Primary School, Kelty

THE MILLENNIUM 2000

Millennium is here
So let's have a cheer
The kids drink cola
The grown-ups drink beer
Cake, juice, buns
Mmm, over here.
Millennium is here
So let's have a cheer
For the new year.

Claire Ednie (10)
St Joseph's Primary School, Kelty

MY LITTLE SECRET

My little secret is under my bed,
there's a hairy monster with a funny head.
He comes out at night when we're all fast asleep,
he goes into the cupboard to have something to eat.

But one night as I was sleeping, I heard someone shout,
so I looked out of my window and saw him running about.
I tried to bring him back but he ran away,
I've never seen him since that sad day.

Samantha McCulloch (10)
St Joseph's Primary School, Kelty

THE FIRST DAY OF A GIRAFFE'S LIFE

Born at six feet
Towering over the zoo wall.
So many people gathering around the stall
When the big door opens,
Snorting and puffing,
Out it goes.

Blinding sun upon its eyes,
Trying to get to his mother to suckle.
Side by side they stick like glue,
The day is nearly over.

They go inside
The giraffe is exhausted
Then they nod off
Together.

Jason Moffat (10)
St Joseph's Primary School, Kelty

My Little Hamster

My little hamster is
cute and furry

He slurps all day
and he runs in
a hurry

I don't know why
but anyway

He is my hamster
and I'm going to say
I love to play
with my little hamster
as long as he plays too.

James Gill (10)
St Joseph's Primary School, Kelty

CELEBRATION 2000

Dancing dogs and drums go boom
We'll start the millennium very soon.
Trumpets blowing horses go wild
Some of the girls are very mild
Look at that boy jumping up and down
Clowns are telling the news at town
People come from near and far
Instead of walking they take the car
So let's celebrate this celebration
While we've got the invitation.

Claire Donaldson (9)
St Joseph's Primary School, Kelty

DOLPHINS

The dolphin tries to reach the sky
But always fails and starts to cry.
I wish I was a dolphin too
I would just swim about in the blue
In the future I want to swim with dolphins
But I will always admire them.

Megan Webb (9)
St Joseph's Primary School, Kelty

PINK BLOSSOM, WHITE SNOW

She was born in spring,
She was born on a blossom day,
She had a husband who was old too.
The night was getting darker,
It was a white winter.

Virginia Cayzer (9)
St Katharine's School, St Andrews

A Picture Of Old Age

A Pipe, a pair of glasses, a walking stick,
a pair of tatty slippers all lay by the fire.
Behind them an old man in a comfy chair
with a Scotsman on his lap,
but he is not reading. He is asleep.
He wakes to the smell of piping hot soup
and fresh bread,
put on the table by his frail wife.
Sitting down they talk about what
they should buy their grandchildren for
Christmas
because as you know
old people spoil their grandchildren.

After consuming all the soup and suggestions
they sit in front of the television
sipping a mug of cocoa.
It is getting late so when they have finished
their cocoa
they go and snuggle down in bed.

That is what I think about when
I think of old age.
What do you think about?

Emily Ventress (11)
St Katharine's School, St Andrews

TRYING TO BE YOUNG AGAIN

My granny loves working in the kitchen,
My sister and I always get spoilt.
My granny loves to watch us playing games,
She never feels left out.
She tries to play football,
But cannot run fast enough.
She tries to play tennis,
But misses the ball.

If she stopped trying,
It would be less fun.

I love my granny,
She's cool.

Hilary Myles (11)
St Katharine's School, St Andrews

BE HAPPY

When you're old and grey,
And start to fade away,
You have yellow teeth,
And a bad memory.

Think of your grandchildren,
Your misspent youth.
Running up and down the village
Diving in that freezing swimming pool,
Staying up all night partying.

So now you are older, just
Be happy.

Katrina Nancy Larson (11)
St Katharine's School, St Andrews

OLD GRANDPA

Toddle toddle toddle
down the road he goes
to get his toffees and his newspaper.
Hop into the car and go to the garden centre,
have a cake and a cup of tea,
go and visit Dave for a natter
so that Dave can catch up on all the news.
Homeward bound then to bed.

Rachael Drummond (11)
St Katharine's School, St Andrews

MY GRANDPA'S WORK!

My grandpa worked for a school,
A school my grandpa worked for.
But every time he went to school,
He forgot the keys to the door.
He forgot the keys to the classroom,
Every time he went to school,
The headmaster kicked him out of the door,
And he landed in a pool.

My grandpa worked as a vet,
As a vet my grandpa worked for,
So many crazy animals,
Like the lion, giraffe and boar.
He got so bored of animals,
Like the lion, giraffe and boar,
He wanted a different career,
He wanted something more.

By this time he became old,
He became old by this time,
I like him this way I see him,
It's like he's even mine.
We all get to see him more,
Mummy, Granny and I,
Even though he's very poor,
I think he deserves *more!*

Lynnette Nicholson (11)
St Katharine's School, St Andrews

THE OLD LADY

Sitting in the grass by the trees
What a wrinkly face like the bark of trees
With a cotton hat and thick grey baggy tights
With her black bag in her hands
Her scarf on too
Short hair like string or cord
Sandal-like shoes with holes in them
Her small ears with wrinkles on them
And pink fat lips like a strawberry
Picking mushrooms in the green forest
With black and white Dalmatian clothes
Her wedding ring in the colour of honey
All in black
A widow.

Emma Barclay (8)
St Katharine's School, St Andrews

OLD

Small like a child,
Thick short grey hair.
Bright blue eyes,
Small button nose.
Wrinkles everywhere,
Bumpy skin like leaves,
Old musty smell like an old wardrobe.
Inside, warm like a kettle,
Outside, cold like a fridge.

A kind loving person,
Just old.

Merle Henderson (8)
St Katharine's School, St Andrews

BECAUSE

My gran can't hear very well
Because she is old
She can't see very well
Because she is old
She puts far too much salt in her food
Because she is old
She is so delicate
Because she is old.

My gran feels quite happy
In the spring
Because everybody else is in the street
So my gran smiles
My gran loves the summer
Because she does not have to worry
About being cold as much as she used to.
The summer cheers her up

Gran thinks it is quite pretty in the autumn
Because she likes watching the leaves fall off the trees
But she would not like to go out of the house.
My gran hates winter
Because she is just sitting by her fire inside all day
She feels very lonely.

Poppy Open (9)
St Katharine's School, St Andrews

DESERT TREE

Old, ancient tree,
Nobody could ever match its age,
Twisty and wrinkled life,
Like an old lady,
Leaves all gone,
Stripped bare,
Only its rough old bark to cover it,
Cover up its expiring secrets to all the world,
It will not always stand,
It will soon fall down.

Eleanor Affleck (9)
St Katharine's School, St Andrews

WHO AM I?

I have hair as grey as rain clouds,
I have lines like old snakes.
I sit in a silk chair that I got when I was young,
It reminds me of the past.
When I am not reading the newspaper,
I watch the television.
I can't run and walk like I used to,
So I sit in my chair.
Who am I?

Alexandra Addison-Scott (8)
St Katharine's School, St Andrews

BAND OF GOLD

With wrinkles and white hair
Sitting with her green dress
And a purple hat on
Thinking of the past.

Dreams floating by
Winter dreams in fact
With her pearls round her neck
In her rocking chair.

Rocking with hands on lap
Dim blue eyes twinkling
As she sits thinking
About her band of gold.

Louise Easton (10)
St Katharine's School, St Andrews

MY GREAT GRANNIE

My Grannie is so very nice,
She gives me lots of love.
When I stay at her big house,
We keep ourselves cosy and warm all night.

I love my Grannie because,
She is well experienced at everything.
Grannie has a long crooked stick,
Elegant spectacles and a very big heart.

When she comes to my house,
We have a great time.
We do a puzzle with 1000 pieces.
It takes us all night.

My Grannie is my Great Grannie.

Katy Craig (9)
St Katharine's School, St Andrews

WHEN I AM OLD

When I am old I will not sit by the fire,
Knitting or watching a boring gardening programme,
Or have a tiny little sweet dog.

I will be up the highest mountain,
My eyelashes will be frozen together but,
I will be wearing a sleeveless T-shirt and some shorts,
Have a German Shepherd who is so fierce that,
I will not be able to touch or go near it.

I won't eat my greens or have morning tea and biscuits,
I'll live on crisps and Coke,
Wear baggy jeans and a sparkly jumper.

I won't spend my pension money on shopping or taxes,
I definitely will not drive a car,
All my pension money will be spent on beer and champagne,
I'll drive at 160 miles an hour,
On a Harley Davidson motorbike,

I will never sleep,
Yet I shall be as pretty,
As a tree in spring.

But I think that perhaps,
Just one or two of my ambitions are just,
Maybe a little tiny bit too ambitious,
So when I'm old,
I'll be who I feel.

Sarah Hartland-Mahon (11)
St Katharine's School, St Andrews

AUTUMN

The green grass, the orange leaves, the brown soil,
all in one day.
It smells earthy and autumny also cold, cold as ice.

The rain falls, the trees stay stock-still.
Birds twitter,
then the air is silent.

Geese fly by
bushes drip
leaves fall.
The soil smells damp
and time goes on and on.

Katrina Affleck (10)
St Katharine's School, St Andrews

ROCKING SWING

A swinging chair like a clock's pendulum,
Steadily going right and left.
A swing, rocking back and forth in the wind.

An old lady sits on the swing,
She does not swing
As she is too frail and weak.
She sits just moving when a gust of wind
Blows the swing very gently.
As she swings she keeps the slow rhythm
Sometimes there's a creak of the chain
But other than that
Silence.

Fiona Hendrie (11)
St Katharine's School, St Andrews

TWO OLD CHARGERS

Two old men sitting on a park bench
Watching the children running
Thinking back to scoring a century,
His Triumph Herald and how things have changed.

No worries just staying chomping the grass
Dreaming
Reminiscing
Talking to old friends
Discussing old rides
The lovely streams, the shows, the crowds
The victory gallops,
The huge jumps, the rosettes,
Watching the young horses and ponies playing
The cheeky little ponies racing up the field
Thinking back to when they played and raced.

Camilla Beaton (11)
St Katharine's School, St Andrews

THE FALSE TEETH MONSTER

There is a monster in Grandad's room
I can see it in the gloom
It goes chitter-chatter
My heart goes pitter-patter

It lives in a glass on the shelf
My brother thinks it's an elf
I know it's a scary monster though
He might eat children, you never know

In the morning the light is on
The scary monster has suddenly gone
Then I realise, what a relief
The scary monster was Grandad's false teeth.

Joanna Brown (8)
St Katharine's School, St Andrews

MY SPECIAL GRANDMA

My grandma has looked after me,
Since my mummy died.
It was very sad for me,
As I was only five.

She bathed me and dressed me,
And fed me through the day,
At night she read me stories,
Like Pooky and Jackana,
And stroked my head and talked to me,
Until I went to sleep.

And now that she has married my step-grandpa,
I live with them for good.
With my very own room,
And my very own cat
And a garden by the brae
And a summerhouse full of toys,
Where my sister and I can play.
I love her very much you see,
Although they are getting old,
I think she is lovely and looks nice too,
I would not change her for the world.
I've told and told and told.

Rachel Coleman (8)
St Katharine's School, St Andrews

OLD TOYS

I'm old and very sad
It makes me feel sad
I have one eye that always cries
When it has to say goodbye to other toys.
My ears are broken up
So I can't hear all the wonderful sounds
It breaks my heart when new toys come in
With lovely new eyes that can see
And ears that can hear.

Alexandra Lindesay Bethune (10)
St Katharine's School, St Andrews

AULD WIFIE FRAE CRAIL

There wis an auld wifie frae Crail,
Wi' a girth 'boot the size o' a whale,
Her weight wis a crime,
So she's servin' her time,
She'll only juist fit in the jail!

Emily Roff (11)
St Katharine's School, St Andrews

THE FIREWORK PARTY

Fireworks, powerful, hot, bright,
Explosive, big bang, sparkle, fright,
Glitter in the moonlight, entertaining me,
'Got to get home, time for tea.'

Dangerous, dark, quiet, then noise!
The children crying, cuddling their toys,
Sleepy people next to me,
'Got to get home, time for tea.'

The party is over, the clock strikes nine,
Everyone starts walking, they look at the time,
Tired, yawning, it's finished, we're told,
'Got to get home, my food is cold.'

Margaret Houston (10)
St Katharine's School, St Andrews

BLUE

Blue is the ocean
Blue is the sea
Blue is the sky above my face
Filled with glee.
Blue is the sky on a sunny day
When everyone is at the bay
Blue is the blue tit sitting in the tree
Blue is the ocean
Blue is the sea.

Heloise Thomson (9)
St Katharine's School, St Andrews

MY DREAMS FOR THE FUTURE

In the future I would like
to be a nurse.
I would like to have
two children one day,
I would like two girls
and I would call them
Gillian and Jemma,
I would also like to go to
California.

Lynsay Hutton (12)
St Serf's Primary School, High Valleyfield

IN THE FUTURE I HOPE FOR

In the future I hope
to be a midwife.
I would like a little boy and girl
and I would call them
Caitlin and Josh.
I would also like to
travel the world.

Gillian Young (11)
St Serf's Primary School, High Valleyfield

ABOUT MY FUTURE

I want to have lots of money,
and a big house.
I would like to live in Florida.
When I grow up
I would like to be a beautician.
I would like to meet all the stars from TV
I would love to meet the people from Friends too.
If I don't have lots of money,
I would like to win the lottery.

Meggan Dunlop (11)
St Serf's Primary School, High Valleyfield

THE YEAR 2000

The year 2000 is a year away,
It gets closer every day,
When it gets here there'll be a big cheer,
And celebrations will get underway.

During the build up,
There're a lot of preparations,
The Millennium Dome needs a lot of certifications,
The builders will say 'Is this OK?'
The designers reply 'There's not enough time.'

The Millennium Bug will wreck our PCs,
We need lots of money to get rid of the disease,
On our computers the date needs to change,
Or they will be plunged into craze.

And that sums it up,
Apart from one thing,
And that is the change that it will bring,
But somehow we'll cope, life isn't a game,
1000 years before we do it again.

Matthew Evans (12)
Strathdevon Primary School

A NEW MILLENNIUM

The sign on the Forth Bridge day by day,
Shows the millennium's not too far away,
Machines break down just overnight,
Dodgy traffic lights giving off the wrong light.

The Millennium Dome won't be ready on time,
Workers still slaving into the grime,
Inside there's going to be a load of cool stuff,
The question is 'Is there time enough?'

The millennium will bring celebrations galore,
With parties and riots that are quite uncalled for,
1000 years are nearly at an end,
Hope that my clock which the bug wrecks, will mend.

Philip Davenport (11)
Strathdevon Primary School

FIRST FLIGHT

Look over,
What do you see?
It's time to go,
Don't you agree?
It's not a case of you following me,
Just jump and flap,
And don't fall out,
If you do,
Just give me a shout.

You fell,
Oh well,
That's OK,
We can try again another day.

Ashley Mackenzie (12)
Strathdevon Primary School

A Winter's Day

The fresh fluffy snow lies on the ground
The pearly white colour covers the world
Marbling patterns take over the windows
Pure Arctic snowballs are waiting to be made
Crunching footsteps are coming near
The stillness is waiting to be disturbed
Delicate crystals on the spider's web.

Jessica Smith (11)
Strathdevon Primary School

SPARKLES OF ICE

The sparkly snowflakes lay on the cars,
Frozen ponds and puddles where children slip and slide,
Frosty old grass in the park,
Hard as stone could be.
The glittering signs and frosted roofs,
The slippery back road where I play about.
When it's frosty it brightens up the light of day,
Until the sun goes down.
The next day I hope for snow as well as slippery roads.
Frosty trees which remind me of Christmas,
As they dazzle in the sun,
Not only this but gardens too,
The playground toys that sit there tranquil and serene.
The glitters of day down into the night
Last for hours and hours.
The freezing weather which makes me wrap up,
In all my warm winter woollies,
The children playing winter games
And slipping in the puddles.

Sarah Witham (11)
Strathdevon Primary School

IN 50 YEARS' TIME

In 50 years' time where will you be,
Protecting the planet or under the sea,
Singing or dancing or making the tea,
In 50 years' time where will you be?

In 50 years' time what will you do,
If there's no food left and it's because of you,
If everyone's crying, with nothing to do,
In 50 years' time what will you do?

Kim Allison (11)
Strathdevon Primary School

2001

It's coming close to twelve o'clock,
Where will you be when the bells go off,
Dancing in space with aliens from Mars,
Or jumping for joy right up to the stars.
Will you be flying on brand new bikes?
With magical planes that take seconds in flight,
Maybe you'll be wearing metal clothes,
Where will you be nobody knows.

What will you do when the bells are ringing,
Will you be happy and jumping and singing?
Whatever you do in 2001,
Make sure it's in Scotland where we'll have the best
Millennium.

Kirsty Lamond (11)
Strathdevon Primary School

WINTER

The morning is fresh and still
It's too quiet and tranquil for me.
So I look out the window and see,
My world has been transformed.
It's covered by a blanket of snow
It's unreal.

Meagan McConnachie (11)
Strathdevon Primary School

LIFE CYCLE

Egg laid
Bird made

Egg cracking
Bird hatching

Insect killing
Mouth filling

First flight
Out of sight

Leaving home
Building own

Finding a mate
Laying eight

Then the story
Begins again!

Claire Turner (11)
Strathdevon Primary School

FREEDOM TO FLY

A bird has the freedom to fly
In the sky
It needs no passport or ticket
Its wings are its passport to fly
In the sky
And go anywhere
Do anything.

Diving, swooping whatever they do
You know they'll be watching me and you
To see the world from a different view
No barriers for them just for me and you
A bird has the freedom to fly
In the sky.

Gliding along in the air so high
Looking at everything going by
Their sharp beady eyes
Looking out for some food
Spotted a mouse, no make that two
A bird has the freedom to fly
In the sky.

Skimming along the water for some food
Sleeping in nests and bushes
The birds see the world from a different view
No barriers for them just for me and you
A bird has the freedom to fly
In the sky.

Alison Cockerton (12)
Strathdevon Primary School

THE NIGHT

The night is like a deep dark hole,
Waiting to swallow me up.
I lie in bed thinking,
What will happen to me.
The owls toot in rhythm,
To the howling of the wolves
And the moon is like an eye,
Watching down on me.

Carolyn Stewart (11)
Strathdevon Primary School

Money, Money, Money!

Goggles are for swimming,
  Bats are for cricket,
    Spikes are for running,
      Money, money, spend, spend!

Racquets are for badminton,
  Trainers are for football,
    Blades are for skating on,
      Money, money, spend, spend!

Ashley Hyde (11)
Strathdevon Primary School

THE LITTLE MOLE

Under the ground of a wheat field,
A lonely little mole dug a tunnel.
He dug all day, and half the night.

Up he popped, out of his tunnel,
Then he met a fluffy brown rabbit,
The rabbit hopped away, and lay in his burrow.

Across the field the mole ran,
He met a little field mouse.
The field mouse showed the mole his house,
And then ran away.

Through the field the mole ran,
Looking for a good place to dig,
He dug again, then went to sleep in
His newly built tunnel.

Nicola Kidd (9)
Tayport Primary School

THE WILD HORSE

Behind the farm,
The wild horse runs,
For a thunderstorm to come.

Below the trees it stomps and runs,
It really wants a storm to come,
I wouldn't like to get too close
He seems to be in a bad mood.

Over and under the fence it runs,
Out of sight in the dark,
He seems really angry now.

Inside it's quiet,
But then the storm starts
And now the horse is happy
And the family aren't.

Roisin Connolly (9)
Tayport Primary School

THE DOGS IN CRUFTS

Around, close to the audience,
The boxer dog looks very smart.
Walking smartly
Now he is running very fast.

On the seesaw carefully
The poodle goes down the swing
Very carefully
Now off she runs close to the audience.

Inside the tunnel the alsatian goes.
Outside the tunnel.
Now close to the audience.
Look how he walks.

Through the tunnel the Lassie dog goes.
She is on the seesaw
Now she is finished.
Now she is close to the audience
Look how she runs.
Now she is walking nice and steady.

Sonali Jayasekera (10)
Tayport Primary School

EASTER

E   veryone having fun
A   nyone gets and egg or two
S   ure you get Easter eggs
T   elling nobody what you get
E   veryone enjoys Easter
R   oaring or giggling children on Easter day.

Rebecca Anderson (9)
Tayport Primary School

MY DOG

Behind the sofa my dog is sleeping,
Out I come not knowing where to look for him,
I shout for him, he walks away,
I look behind the sofa, he's not there.

Under the table he goes scuttling,
He thinks I am going to smack him,
I call him out, he licks my face.

Off we go to play in the garden,
We play with the ball,
And I take him for a walk.

Kayleigh Hunter (9)
Tayport Primary School

EASTER

E   aster is coming closer each day,
A   ll the children are waiting for the day to come,
S   amantha the rabbit has to wait till 4th April,
T   ill Easter is here I won't get any chocolate,
E   aster is a happy day, Easter is a funny day too,
R   abbits like Easter and so do lots of children.

Nicola Rennie (9)
Tayport Primary School

HIDING

Under the ground the rabbits sleep,
All huddled up,
In a heap.

Under the leaves
The hedgehogs hide,
All warm and round.

In the house,
All cosy and warm,
There is me and you and everyone.

Hannah Grant (9)
Tayport Primary School

THE LITTLE LIZARD

Underneath a cold damp stone,
A hungry lizard lay,
He thought of all the lovely flies,
Dreams of sunny days.

He lay in the darkness,
Thinking of fat flies,
He stuck out his tongue,
'Ahh' he shouted, 'rain!'

He ran and ran,
Until he found shelter,
Then he went to sleep,
And when he woke up,
It was summer.

He ran about chasing all the fat flies,
Then he bumped into the fattest fly he had ever seen,
He gobbled it up in one go,
That was the end of the fat fly.

Katrina Reid (9)
Tayport Primary School

BIRTHDAY

B rilliant, cool, wow!
I t's my birthday,
R emember my birthday cake,
T hink of all the things I'll get,
H ave some cake,
D ance, let's dance,
A fter all that, I'm really tired.
Y awning slightly now, I'm fast asleep zzzzz...

Kimberley Lawson (9)
Tayport Primary School

NIGHT

Night is scary, creepy and silent,
I don't like the night.
Ghosts come out,
'Ha ha' goes the ghost,
Tapping at the window.

Maria Lindsay (9)
Tayport Primary School

DOLPHINS

D olphins are wonderful animals,
O n the sparkling water,
L eaping in the air,
P eople come to see them dance,
H elping other dolphins,
I n under the sandy water,
N ow you see them swimming,
S ome dolphins are shy.

Joanne McCormick (9)
Tayport Primary School

THE WORLD

Under the cold, wet, ground,
Lay a wise old badger,
Thinking how the world was made.

Outside, he listened to the wind,
Howling and whirling,
Leaves are in the air.

Out I come from my hole,
It is cold and windy,
I still wonder how the world was made.

Catriona Swanston (9)
Tayport Primary School

Rabbit Adventure

In its hutch sits the rabbit,
Worrying when sunny days come,
Its hutch is full of food.

Out of its hutch it runs about,
Food and water is what he goes for,
When he drinks the water and eats the food, he's in his hutch.

Over the roof of his hutch he goes,
The hutch is full of food,
He is a very good rabbit.

David Leitch (9)
Tayport Primary School

HORSES

H   orses are wild things,
O   ver the poles they jump,
R   unning round the field,
S   houting out *neigh!*
E   verbody loves them,
S   ee how they jump.

Ashley Clark (9)
Tayport Primary School

THE GREAT MUSICIAN

B eethoven was a great musician,
E njoyable music he played with pleasure,
E xciting, loud and marvellous,
T apping away on his beautiful piano,
H appy with his famous life,
O ut and in the music hall,
V icious he wasn't, but kind he was,
E xpert with the rest of the orchestra,
N erve he hadn't, but talented he was.

Iain Anderson (9)
Tayport Primary School

AN ANT'S LIFE

Under the ground,
The tiny ants are building their home,
While above the ground,
The other ants are collecting food.

Behind the ants that are collecting the food,
A beetle is waiting to pounce on the unexpecting ant,
While behind the beetle,
Is a whole army of ants.

Above the ants in the air is a bird,
Looking for an insect for her chicks,
The ants below her are scurrying away back to their colony,
In case she decides they would make a good meal.

Owen Bissett (9)
Tayport Primary School

EASTER

E aster is here, let's have some fun,
A s Jesus rolls his rock and comes free,
S chool is out, so let's have fun,
T ummy pain is no good, we want to eat,
E aster eggs all around, good for us to eat,
R elax, we're out of school, no more homework, yes!

Sam Harte (10)
Tayport Primary School

AUTUMN IS HERE

In the burrow, damp and cold, the rabbit thinks of wintry days still
to come,
The foxes and badgers still out hunting,
The hedgehog already in hibernation,
The vole and otter, still looking for food.

The beetles making a mighty city of mud and rabbit dung,
The skunks hibernating and the badgers are now,
Bees and wasps have already died.

The amphibians looking for somewhere to live,
The bears in their caves and away to sleep for three or four months now,
That's a long time.
Birds in their nests, the blackbirds watching the sparks of fireworks
everywhere,
A few more months to go, now I wonder if the squirrel has got
the acorns,
I hope every animal has got all the food that it needs for the winter.

Michael Fitchet (9)
Tayport Primary School

RIVERS

R ivers meandering,
I n Scotland by the ocean,
V the river looks like a 'V',
E rosion, I know what that means,
R iver Nile is the biggest in the world,
S everal rivers all throughout Britain.

Martin Fearn (9)
Tayport Primary School

ANIMALS IN THE PARK

Over the trees the blue tit cheeps,
Behind the oak,
Across from the park.

Below the oak, the ant hill stands,
Next to the oak, but busy ants work,
In the park I sit and watch them work.

Next to the park my house stands,
Through the park I run,
Hearing all the happy birds cheep.

Robbie Welsh (9)
Tayport Primary School

THE YUMMY MEAL

Behind the fence,
Was a snake,
On a rock coloured red.

Beneath the shed,
Something moved,
That something was a beetle.

The snake slithered over,
The beetle was dead,
It did not stand a chance,
Because the snake was the best!

Ewan Millar (10)
Tayport Primary School

DOWN IN THE JUNGLE

Down in the jungle a monkey lived,
The hunters tried to catch him, but he was too quick.

Down in the jungle a monkey lived,
He played chase with the tigers and tig with his kids.

Down in the jungle a monkey lived,
He put his kids to bed, and collapsed on his head.

Mathew Leslie (10)
Tayport Primary School

A Summer In The Sun

Outside in the sun,
A dog sleeps through the day,
Thinking of all the bones on their way.

Behind the hedgerow,
A cat purrs happily away,
When its kittens play in the sun.

Above their heads, chicks sing noisily,
Knowing their mother is on the way,
Coming through the clouds as white as whey.

Coll Graham (9)
Tayport Primary School

Sassy

I once knew a cat called Sassy,
Who I thought was classy,
She is soft and cuddly,
And likes her bath bubbly.

She is black and white,
And does not bite,
She is fluffy
And very puffy.

She has a friend called Taz,
And I have a friend called Shaz,
Although my cat Sassy is strange,
I love her.

Domenica Reilly (11)
Wellwood Primary School

THE BATTLE OF CULLODEN

I hoped I wouldn't get slaughtered,
I killed many warriors,
The blood gushed all over the battlefield,
The noise of the guns,
Almost burst my ear drums,
I had to run for miles,
We lost the battle.

Gary Dudley (10)
Wellwood Primary School

MY DREAM

My dream is to be a footballer,
I would love to play for Manchester United,
I think Pelé is the world's best ever player,
It would be great to follow in his footsteps,
It would be amazing to be the captain,
And lead the team to glory,
My dream is to be a footballer.

Lee Paterson (11)
Wellwood Primary School

HOME

It is in a small village where
Everyone is so nice that I live,
It gives me a bed and warmth,
It gives me TV,
It is my home sweet home.

Danny Russell (11)
Wellwood Primary School

MUM

My love is great,
The most I could create,
From the start,
You were in my heart,
I love you so,
From head to toe,
You're the best ever,
Couldn't get one like you, never ever,
I'm growing up every day,
But I'll always love you in every way,
You're always my friend,
I'll love you till the very end.

Charlene Stewart (11)
Wellwood Primary School

MILLENNIUM

The millennium is coming,
Celebrations and laughter,
People are shaking hands,
The bells on Big Ben
Strike twelve. *Hip hip hip hurrah!*
It has reached the year 2000.
People are street-partying.
Music is blaring,
The streets are crowded,
Animals are hibernating.

Stephen Lynch (11)
Wormit Primary School

MILLENNIUM

The millennium is coming,
Excitement fills the air,
Celebrations will soon be here,
People will be singing everywhere,
It will bring smiles to people's faces,
Who will be shaking hands,
Hands will be shaking everywhere,
In every single land,
The millennium is coming,
And everyone will be excited,
The clock will strike twelve,
And everyone will be reunited.

Michael Truscott (11)
Wormit Primary School

PARTY 2000

Aliens come from far and beyond,
Just to see what's going on.
They party on through the night,
And give the humans quite a fright.
The birds and the bees,
And the flowers and the trees,
Jump up and dance till they've got sore knees,
Drinking and singing,
And dancing and prancing,
The bell chimes twelve for the new year,
And people round the world shout and cheer.

Roger Carter (11)
Wormit Primary School

THE MILLENNIUM

M any people celebrate the millennium, a new decade, a new
    century, a new decade.

I n streets, in houses, people are cheering and rejoicing.

L ights go on all over the country, making it look beautiful.

L ands all over the world celebrate with us.

E nding is part of the millennium. We say goodbye to '99, the 20th
    century, and the last millennium.

N ight falls and the millennium draws closer, closer,

N ine minutes to go. People hold their breath, waiting.

I magine the happiness everywhere, people laughing and dancing.

U sually we celebrate the millennium, every thousand years. Now we
    are counting, five, four, three, two, one.

M illennium is here!

Katy Gadd (11)
Wormit Primary School

MILLENNIUM

Jolly men and women fill
The streets of Edinburgh,
The clock strikes twelve o'clock,
Hurray!
It's the year 2000,
Cries come from the crowd,
And fireworks begin.
Cheers from living rooms,
People shaking hands as
They forget all the bad times,
A new beginning, a new millennium.

Carrie Millar (11)
Wormit Primary School

MILLENNIUM WILDLIFE

The sleek, grey shapes of dolphins,
Dip in and out of choppy waves,
Free to roam the waters.
Squirrels prance up the tall spruce trees,
Racing up the trunks like a clockwork mouse.
Rainbow-coloured parrots squawk,
As they fly through the treetops of their home,
The rainforest.
On the dusty plains of Africa, the lions
Do not flick an eyelid as the flies
Buzz around their face.
Suddenly disaster strikes!
Whales are hunted and shot,
Rainforests are cut down without a care,
No longer does the parrot squawk,
The lion roar, the monkeys talk.
The forest where the squirrel used to roam,
Is now gone.
Will this change in the millennium?

Natalie Weir (11)
Wormit Primary School

PARTY

Getting ready,
Going out,
Having fun,
Disco dancing,
Celebrating,
Countdown starts,
Clock strikes twelve,
Cheering crowds,
New beginnings,
Resolutions.

Darren Smith (11)
Wormit Primary School

THE MILLENNIUM

Will war break out in the year 2000
Or will there be peace instead?
Will human beings grow up?
Will third world countries be fed?
Will animal rights be understood
Or will extinction be world-wide?
Will the countries be united?
Will there be new light?
Will all poverty be abolished
Or will pollution never end?
Will humans be forgotten?
Will the millennium be the end?

Gillian Paterson (11)
Wormit Primary School

MILLENNIUM

The millennium is a speedy cheetah,
Racing for its tea.
The millennium is a time bomb exploding.
The millennium is trips up to space all day,
To see the planets.
The millennium is volcanoes erupting endlessly.
The millennium is fireworks,
Exploding for hours.

Gemma Barclay (11)
Wormit Primary School

THE MILLENNIUM BUG

I'm trying to catch the Millennium Bug,
Before it's New Year's Eve,
But I can't even find it so,
I don't think I'll achieve.
It'll eat up computers and tape recorders too,
And microwaves and ovens,
Just to spite you.
I laid a trap for it in Kinbrae park,
But I haven't trapped it yet,
I even tried waiting in the cold and dark,
With my green and blue fishing net.
It'll eat up computers and tape recorders too,
And microwaves and ovens,
Just to spite you.
It's said to be spotty with pink and red wings,
But I don't think that is true,
Don't ask me what I think it is,
'Cause I don't have a clue.
It'll eat up computers and tape recorders too,
And microwaves and ovens,
Just to spite you.
The year 2000's coming up,
And I haven't caught the bug yet,
But I will catch it before that day,
And be famous in Britain I bet!

Amy Downes (11)
Wormit Primary School

MILLENNIUM

M assive party at my house, going on all night,
I n the morning feeling all drowsy and light,
L ike a fast cheetah racing away,
L ike a slow slug when you wake up the next day,
E xcitement goes on as everyone drinks beer,
N othing is heard but laughter and cheer,
N o one's in bed they are all up partying,
I maginations run wild while everyone's smiling,
U nbelievable fireworks going off in the sky,
M orning comes and everyone says goodbye.

Robert Crombie (11)
Wormit Primary School

THE MILLENNIUM IS HERE

Hip hip, hooray!
The millennium is here,
I wonder what will happen,
This very fine year.
Will there be laughter,
And good cheer,
Or will there be gloom and despair?
I hope that they don't
Cut down more trees,
And I hope they stop
Polluting the seas,
I hope everything turns out well,
So Happy Millennium everyone,
I wish you all well.

Andrew Truscott (11)
Wormit Primary School

THE MILLENNIUM BUG

I am sitting at my window,
Looking at the street,
Seeing all the people,
And the people that they meet.

Sitting at my window,
In the middle of the town,
I see children playing,
If only I look down.

Still sitting at my window,
Things get more exciting,
The Millennium Bug has got me,
And really it's quite frightening.

I'm not sitting at my window,
I am playing with a friend,
My friend is having a party,
But all celebrations have to end.

I am sitting at the window,
The window of the bus,
My wheelchair is folded in the back,
Because the driver made a fuss.

I am sitting at my window,
Looking at the park,
Thinking I should be there,
Before my life gets dark.

Clea Russell (11)
Wormit Primary School

IRAQ BOMBING

Last night it was my turn,
They came and bombed the house down.
They killed my mother and father,
And buried what was left on the ground.
So I go walking homeless.
They spend money on their families,
But there's nothing left for me.
So I'll just keep being homeless,
Till someone notices me.

Nicole Webber (11)
Wormit Primary School

MILLENNIUM

Happy New Year say the people,
It's a new beginning,
It's the millennium,
Excitement turns as the clock strikes twelve,
People make new year resolutions,
It's the millennium.
All you can hear is laughter,
We have parties and drinks.
It's the millennium.
People make new friends,
They visit the Dome,
It's the millennium.
People feast on cheese and pickles,
But still ignore hunger and thirst,
It's the millennium.

Samantha Young (11)
Wormit Primary School

MILLENNIUM

The millennium is coming,
Everyone is celebrating apart from the tramps lying in the dirt,
No celebrations for them.
Parties are going on, everyone is so happy.
They have waited long for this day.
The tramp hasn't waited long for this day,
It's just another normal day on the street for them,
Looking for scraps of food, sleeping in shop doorways.
People are enjoying the lovely food and
Having the most wonderful time.
To celebrate the millennium, the tramps has found
Half a chicken roll.

Jennifer Rourke (12)
Wormit Primary School

MILLENNIUM

Millennium is coming to celebrate with us,
Millennium, it is the time to party all round,
Millennium is the music blaring away,
Millennium is the drink getting thrown away,
Millennium is people eating the food,
Millennium, it is the people having great fun.
Millennium is the bells striking twelve,
A new beginning, the millennium has come.

Emma McRitchie (11)
Wormit Primary School

THE WORM THAT WAS BORN ON THE MILLENNIUM

There was a little worm called Jim,
His life was rather gloom and dim,
All he would do is eat and sleep,
Through his tiny window he could peep,
One morning he said,
'Oh dear, I can't get out of bed'
So little Jim was in his bed all day,
Till his mother slithered his way,
And found out that he had to get an Xray,
The doctor said he'd got a splinter.

Cairo Wilmot (10)
Wormit Primary School

TECHNOLOGY IN THE NEW MILLENNIUM

In the new millennium . . .
We will fly
To school on
Jet-packs.

In the new millennium . . .
We will
Be able,
To time-travel.

In the new millennium . . .
Cars will
Be able to
Fly.

In the new millennium . . .
We will be
Able to live
On other
Planets.

In the new millennium . . .
We will
Be able to
Buy spacesuits.

That's technology in the new millennium.

Ian Brown (11)
Wormit Primary School

MILLENN-HUM

A gorilla growls on the gravel,
A shark shrieks on the shore,
A giraffe jokes around, chewing gum,
But what does a millenni - hum?

Ponies play pianos like some puddle ducks,
An orang-utan plays the organ,
While trying to open trucks,
A wolf whistles while walking with his chum,
But what does a millenni - hum?

A spider sings sweetly in the sauna,
A dormouse drowns him out with the drums,
A tiger tunes his tenor on time,
But what does a millenni,
What does a millenni,
What does a millenni - hum?

Lesley Aitken (11)
Wormit Primary School